50 Best Beef Jerky Recipes

By: Kelly Johnson

Table of Contents

- Classic Smoked Beef Jerky
- Teriyaki Beef Jerky
- Spicy Sriracha Beef Jerky
- Honey Garlic Beef Jerky
- Black Pepper and Garlic Beef Jerky
- Maple Bourbon Beef Jerky
- Sweet and Spicy Chili Beef Jerky
- Korean BBQ Beef Jerky
- Smoky Chipotle Beef Jerky
- Pineapple Teriyaki Beef Jerky
- Cajun Spiced Beef Jerky
- Lemon Pepper Beef Jerky
- Hickory Smoked Beef Jerky
- Soy Sauce and Ginger Beef Jerky
- Jalapeño Lime Beef Jerky
- Brown Sugar and Molasses Beef Jerky
- Red Wine Marinated Beef Jerky
- Buffalo-Style Beef Jerky
- Applewood Smoked Beef Jerky
- Curry-Spiced Beef Jerky
- Thai Chili Beef Jerky
- Texas-Style Spicy Beef Jerky
- Beer-Infused Beef Jerky
- Mustard and Honey Beef Jerky
- Sweet Mesquite Beef Jerky
- Garlic Parmesan Beef Jerky
- Espresso Black Pepper Beef Jerky
- Balsamic Vinegar Beef Jerky
- Korean Gochujang Beef Jerky
- Cherrywood Smoked Beef Jerky
- Cranberry-Glazed Beef Jerky
- Bourbon BBQ Beef Jerky
- Pineapple Habanero Beef Jerky
- Chimichurri Beef Jerky
- Dill Pickle Beef Jerky

- Orange Ginger Beef Jerky
- Caribbean Jerk Beef Jerky
- Five-Spice Beef Jerky
- Horseradish and Worcestershire Beef Jerky
- Cilantro Lime Beef Jerky
- Sesame Ginger Beef Jerky
- Tangy Tamarind Beef Jerky
- Firecracker Spicy Beef Jerky
- Cranberry Orange Beef Jerky
- Raspberry Chipotle Beef Jerky
- Mango Chili Beef Jerky
- Hickory Bourbon Beef Jerky
- Smoked Paprika and Honey Beef Jerky
- Lemon Thyme Beef Jerky
- Mediterranean Herb Beef Jerky

Classic Smoked Beef Jerky

Ingredients:

- 2 lbs beef (top round or flank steak)
- ½ cup soy sauce
- 2 tbsp Worcestershire sauce
- 1 tbsp salt
- 1 tbsp black pepper
- 1 tsp garlic powder
- 1 tsp onion powder
- 1 tsp smoked paprika

Instructions:

1. Slice beef into thin strips.
2. Combine marinade ingredients and soak beef for at least 12 hours.
3. Smoke at 160°F (70°C) for 4-6 hours until dry and chewy.

Teriyaki Beef Jerky

Ingredients:

- 2 lbs beef, sliced thin
- ½ cup soy sauce
- ¼ cup honey
- ¼ cup mirin
- 1 tbsp grated ginger
- 2 cloves garlic, minced
- 1 tsp sesame oil
- 1 tsp black pepper

Instructions:

1. Marinate beef in sauce for 12 hours.
2. Smoke or dehydrate at 160°F for 4-6 hours.

Spicy Sriracha Beef Jerky

Ingredients:

- 2 lbs beef, sliced thin
- ½ cup soy sauce
- 3 tbsp Sriracha
- 2 tbsp brown sugar
- 1 tbsp apple cider vinegar
- 1 tsp cayenne pepper

Instructions:

1. Marinate beef overnight.
2. Smoke at 160°F for 4-6 hours.

Honey Garlic Beef Jerky

Ingredients:

- 2 lbs beef, sliced thin
- ½ cup soy sauce
- ¼ cup honey
- 1 tbsp minced garlic
- 1 tbsp Worcestershire sauce
- 1 tsp black pepper

Instructions:

1. Marinate overnight.
2. Smoke at 160°F for 4-6 hours.

Black Pepper and Garlic Beef Jerky

Ingredients:

- 2 lbs beef, sliced thin
- ½ cup soy sauce
- 2 tbsp black pepper
- 1 tbsp garlic powder
- 1 tbsp Worcestershire sauce

Instructions:

1. Marinate overnight.
2. Smoke at 160°F for 4-6 hours.

Maple Bourbon Beef Jerky

Ingredients:

- 2 lbs beef, sliced thin
- ½ cup soy sauce
- ¼ cup maple syrup
- 2 tbsp bourbon
- 1 tbsp black pepper
- 1 tsp smoked paprika

Instructions:

1. Marinate overnight.
2. Smoke at 160°F for 4-6 hours.

Sweet and Spicy Chili Beef Jerky

Ingredients:

- 2 lbs beef, sliced thin
- ½ cup soy sauce
- 2 tbsp honey
- 1 tbsp chili flakes
- 1 tbsp Worcestershire sauce

Instructions:

1. Marinate overnight.
2. Smoke at 160°F for 4-6 hours.

Korean BBQ Beef Jerky

Ingredients:

- 2 lbs beef, sliced thin
- ½ cup soy sauce
- ¼ cup brown sugar
- 1 tbsp gochujang
- 1 tsp sesame oil
- 1 tbsp grated ginger

Instructions:

1. Marinate overnight.
2. Smoke at 160°F for 4-6 hours.

Smoky Chipotle Beef Jerky

Ingredients:

- 2 lbs beef, sliced thin
- ½ cup soy sauce
- 1 tbsp chipotle powder
- 1 tbsp brown sugar
- 1 tbsp smoked paprika

Instructions:

1. Marinate overnight.
2. Smoke at 160°F for 4-6 hours.

Pineapple Teriyaki Beef Jerky

Ingredients:

- 2 lbs beef, sliced thin
- ½ cup pineapple juice
- ½ cup soy sauce
- ¼ cup brown sugar
- 1 tbsp grated ginger

Instructions:

1. Marinate overnight.
2. Smoke at 160°F for 4-6 hours.

Cajun Spiced Beef Jerky

Ingredients:

- 2 lbs beef, sliced thin
- ½ cup soy sauce
- 1 tbsp Cajun seasoning
- 1 tsp cayenne pepper
- 1 tbsp brown sugar

Instructions:

1. Marinate overnight.
2. Smoke at 160°F for 4-6 hours.

Lemon Pepper Beef Jerky

Ingredients:

- 2 lbs beef, thinly sliced
- ½ cup soy sauce
- 1 tbsp lemon zest
- 2 tbsp black pepper
- 1 tbsp honey
- 1 tsp garlic powder
- 1 tbsp lemon juice

Instructions:

1. Marinate beef overnight.
2. Smoke at 160°F (70°C) for 4-6 hours.

Hickory Smoked Beef Jerky

Ingredients:

- 2 lbs beef, thinly sliced
- ½ cup soy sauce
- 1 tbsp hickory liquid smoke
- 2 tbsp Worcestershire sauce
- 1 tbsp smoked paprika
- 1 tbsp brown sugar
- 1 tsp garlic powder

Instructions:

1. Marinate beef overnight.
2. Smoke at 160°F with hickory wood chips for 4-6 hours.

Soy Sauce and Ginger Beef Jerky

Ingredients:

- 2 lbs beef, thinly sliced
- ½ cup soy sauce
- 1 tbsp grated ginger
- 1 tbsp honey
- 1 tbsp sesame oil
- 1 tsp garlic powder

Instructions:

1. Marinate beef overnight.
2. Smoke or dehydrate at 160°F for 4-6 hours.

Jalapeño Lime Beef Jerky

Ingredients:

- 2 lbs beef, thinly sliced
- ½ cup lime juice
- 2 tbsp soy sauce
- 1 fresh jalapeño, finely chopped
- 1 tbsp honey
- 1 tsp salt

Instructions:

1. Marinate overnight.
2. Smoke at 160°F for 4-6 hours.

Brown Sugar and Molasses Beef Jerky

Ingredients:

- 2 lbs beef, thinly sliced
- ½ cup soy sauce
- 2 tbsp brown sugar
- 1 tbsp molasses
- 1 tsp smoked paprika
- 1 tsp black pepper

Instructions:

1. Marinate overnight.
2. Smoke at 160°F for 4-6 hours.

Red Wine Marinated Beef Jerky

Ingredients:

- 2 lbs beef, thinly sliced
- ½ cup red wine
- 2 tbsp soy sauce
- 1 tbsp Worcestershire sauce
- 1 tsp black pepper
- 1 tsp rosemary

Instructions:

1. Marinate overnight.
2. Smoke at 160°F for 4-6 hours.

Buffalo-Style Beef Jerky

Ingredients:

- 2 lbs beef, thinly sliced
- ½ cup hot sauce
- 1 tbsp apple cider vinegar
- 1 tbsp honey
- 1 tsp garlic powder
- 1 tsp cayenne pepper

Instructions:

1. Marinate overnight.
2. Smoke at 160°F for 4-6 hours.

Applewood Smoked Beef Jerky

Ingredients:

- 2 lbs beef, thinly sliced
- ½ cup soy sauce
- 1 tbsp apple cider vinegar
- 1 tbsp brown sugar
- 1 tsp smoked paprika
- 1 tsp black pepper

Instructions:

1. Marinate overnight.
2. Smoke at 160°F with applewood chips for 4-6 hours.

Curry-Spiced Beef Jerky

Ingredients:

- 2 lbs beef, thinly sliced
- ½ cup soy sauce
- 1 tbsp curry powder
- 1 tbsp honey
- 1 tsp garlic powder
- 1 tsp black pepper

Instructions:

1. Marinate overnight.
2. Smoke at 160°F for 4-6 hours.

Thai Chili Beef Jerky

Ingredients:

- 2 lbs beef, thinly sliced
- ½ cup soy sauce
- 1 tbsp fish sauce
- 1 tbsp honey
- 1 tbsp Thai chili flakes
- 1 tsp black pepper

Instructions:

1. Marinate overnight.
2. Smoke at 160°F for 4-6 hours.

Texas-Style Spicy Beef Jerky

Ingredients:

- 2 lbs beef, thinly sliced
- ½ cup soy sauce
- 1 tbsp Worcestershire sauce
- 1 tbsp cayenne pepper
- 1 tbsp black pepper
- 1 tsp smoked paprika

Instructions:

1. Marinate overnight.
2. Smoke at 160°F for 4-6 hours.

Beer-Infused Beef Jerky

Ingredients:

- 2 lbs beef, thinly sliced
- ½ cup dark beer (stout or porter)
- ¼ cup soy sauce
- 1 tbsp Worcestershire sauce
- 1 tbsp brown sugar
- 1 tsp garlic powder
- 1 tsp black pepper

Instructions:

1. Marinate beef in mixture overnight.
2. Smoke or dehydrate at 160°F for 4-6 hours.

Mustard and Honey Beef Jerky

Ingredients:

- 2 lbs beef, thinly sliced
- ½ cup Dijon mustard
- ¼ cup honey
- ¼ cup soy sauce
- 1 tsp garlic powder
- 1 tsp black pepper

Instructions:

1. Marinate overnight.
2. Smoke or dehydrate at 160°F for 4-6 hours.

Sweet Mesquite Beef Jerky

Ingredients:

- 2 lbs beef, thinly sliced
- ½ cup soy sauce
- 2 tbsp mesquite liquid smoke
- 2 tbsp brown sugar
- 1 tsp smoked paprika
- 1 tsp black pepper

Instructions:

1. Marinate overnight.
2. Smoke with mesquite wood at 160°F for 4-6 hours.

Garlic Parmesan Beef Jerky

Ingredients:

- 2 lbs beef, thinly sliced
- ½ cup soy sauce
- 2 tbsp grated Parmesan cheese
- 1 tbsp garlic powder
- 1 tsp black pepper
- 1 tbsp olive oil

Instructions:

1. Marinate overnight.
2. Dehydrate at 160°F for 4-6 hours.

Espresso Black Pepper Beef Jerky

Ingredients:

- 2 lbs beef, thinly sliced
- ½ cup soy sauce
- 2 tbsp brewed espresso
- 1 tbsp brown sugar
- 1 tbsp cracked black pepper
- 1 tsp garlic powder

Instructions:

1. Marinate overnight.
2. Smoke at 160°F for 4-6 hours.

Balsamic Vinegar Beef Jerky

Ingredients:

- 2 lbs beef, thinly sliced
- ½ cup balsamic vinegar
- ¼ cup soy sauce
- 1 tbsp honey
- 1 tsp black pepper
- 1 tsp smoked paprika

Instructions:

1. Marinate overnight.
2. Dehydrate at 160°F for 4-6 hours.

Korean Gochujang Beef Jerky

Ingredients:

- 2 lbs beef, thinly sliced
- ½ cup soy sauce
- 2 tbsp gochujang (Korean chili paste)
- 1 tbsp honey
- 1 tbsp sesame oil
- 1 tsp garlic powder

Instructions:

1. Marinate overnight.
2. Smoke at 160°F for 4-6 hours.

Cherrywood Smoked Beef Jerky

Ingredients:

- 2 lbs beef, thinly sliced
- ½ cup soy sauce
- 1 tbsp honey
- 1 tbsp Worcestershire sauce
- 1 tsp black pepper
- 1 tsp smoked paprika

Instructions:

1. Marinate overnight.
2. Smoke at 160°F with cherrywood chips for 4-6 hours.

Cranberry-Glazed Beef Jerky

Ingredients:

- 2 lbs beef, thinly sliced
- ½ cup cranberry juice
- ¼ cup soy sauce
- 2 tbsp honey
- 1 tsp black pepper
- 1 tsp garlic powder

Instructions:

1. Marinate overnight.
2. Dehydrate at 160°F for 4-6 hours.

Bourbon BBQ Beef Jerky

Ingredients:

- 2 lbs beef, thinly sliced
- ½ cup bourbon
- ¼ cup BBQ sauce
- 1 tbsp brown sugar
- 1 tsp smoked paprika
- 1 tsp garlic powder

Instructions:

1. Marinate overnight.
2. Smoke at 160°F for 4-6 hours.

Pineapple Habanero Beef Jerky

Ingredients:

- 2 lbs beef, thinly sliced
- ½ cup pineapple juice
- 2 tbsp soy sauce
- 1 habanero pepper, finely chopped
- 1 tbsp honey
- 1 tsp black pepper
- 1 tsp garlic powder

Instructions:

1. Marinate overnight.
2. Smoke or dehydrate at 160°F for 4-6 hours.

Chimichurri Beef Jerky

Ingredients:

- 2 lbs beef, thinly sliced
- ½ cup fresh parsley, chopped
- ¼ cup red wine vinegar
- ¼ cup olive oil
- 3 garlic cloves, minced
- 1 tsp crushed red pepper
- 1 tsp salt

Instructions:

1. Blend marinade and soak beef overnight.
2. Dehydrate at 160°F for 4-6 hours.

Dill Pickle Beef Jerky

Ingredients:

- 2 lbs beef, thinly sliced
- ½ cup dill pickle juice
- 2 tbsp soy sauce
- 1 tsp garlic powder
- 1 tsp black pepper
- 1 tsp dried dill

Instructions:

1. Marinate overnight.
2. Dehydrate at 160°F for 4-6 hours.

Orange Ginger Beef Jerky

Ingredients:

- 2 lbs beef, thinly sliced
- ½ cup fresh orange juice
- 2 tbsp soy sauce
- 1 tbsp honey
- 1 tsp grated ginger
- 1 tsp black pepper

Instructions:

1. Marinate overnight.
2. Smoke or dehydrate at 160°F for 4-6 hours.

Caribbean Jerk Beef Jerky

Ingredients:

- 2 lbs beef, thinly sliced
- ½ cup soy sauce
- 1 tbsp brown sugar
- 1 tsp allspice
- ½ tsp cinnamon
- 1 tsp black pepper
- 1 Scotch bonnet pepper, minced

Instructions:

1. Marinate overnight.
2. Smoke at 160°F for 4-6 hours.

Five-Spice Beef Jerky

Ingredients:

- 2 lbs beef, thinly sliced
- ½ cup soy sauce
- 1 tbsp hoisin sauce
- 1 tsp Chinese five-spice powder
- 1 tsp honey
- 1 tsp black pepper

Instructions:

1. Marinate overnight.
2. Dehydrate at 160°F for 4-6 hours.

Horseradish and Worcestershire Beef Jerky

Ingredients:

- 2 lbs beef, thinly sliced
- ½ cup Worcestershire sauce
- 1 tbsp prepared horseradish
- 1 tsp black pepper
- 1 tsp garlic powder

Instructions:

1. Marinate overnight.
2. Smoke or dehydrate at 160°F for 4-6 hours.

Cilantro Lime Beef Jerky

Ingredients:

- 2 lbs beef, thinly sliced
- ½ cup fresh lime juice
- ¼ cup chopped cilantro
- 2 tbsp soy sauce
- 1 tsp black pepper
- 1 tsp garlic powder

Instructions:

1. Marinate overnight.
2. Smoke at 160°F for 4-6 hours.

Sesame Ginger Beef Jerky

Ingredients:

- 2 lbs beef, thinly sliced
- ½ cup soy sauce
- 1 tbsp sesame oil
- 1 tbsp grated ginger
- 1 tsp honey
- 1 tsp black pepper

Instructions:

1. Marinate overnight.
2. Dehydrate at 160°F for 4-6 hours.

Tangy Tamarind Beef Jerky

Ingredients:

- 2 lbs beef, thinly sliced
- ¼ cup tamarind paste
- ¼ cup soy sauce
- 1 tbsp honey
- 1 tsp black pepper
- 1 tsp garlic powder

Instructions:

1. Marinate overnight.
2. Smoke or dehydrate at 160°F for 4-6 hours.

Firecracker Spicy Beef Jerky

Ingredients:

- 2 lbs beef, thinly sliced
- ½ cup soy sauce
- 2 tbsp Sriracha
- 1 tbsp red pepper flakes
- 1 tsp cayenne pepper
- 1 tsp black pepper
- 1 tbsp honey

Instructions:

1. Marinate overnight.
2. Dehydrate at 160°F for 4-6 hours.

Cranberry Orange Beef Jerky

Ingredients:

- 2 lbs beef, thinly sliced
- ½ cup cranberry juice
- ¼ cup fresh orange juice
- 2 tbsp soy sauce
- 1 tbsp honey
- 1 tsp black pepper

Instructions:

1. Marinate overnight.
2. Smoke or dehydrate at 160°F for 4-6 hours.

Raspberry Chipotle Beef Jerky

Ingredients:

- 2 lbs beef, thinly sliced
- ½ cup raspberry puree
- 2 tbsp adobo sauce (from chipotle peppers)
- 2 tbsp soy sauce
- 1 tbsp honey
- 1 tsp garlic powder
- 1 tsp black pepper

Instructions:

1. Marinate overnight.
2. Smoke or dehydrate at 160°F for 4-6 hours.

Mango Chili Beef Jerky

Ingredients:

- 2 lbs beef, thinly sliced
- ½ cup mango puree
- 2 tbsp soy sauce
- 1 tsp chili powder
- 1 tsp smoked paprika
- 1 tbsp honey
- 1 tsp black pepper

Instructions:

1. Marinate overnight.
2. Dehydrate at 160°F for 4-6 hours.

Hickory Bourbon Beef Jerky

Ingredients:

- 2 lbs beef, thinly sliced
- ¼ cup bourbon
- ¼ cup Worcestershire sauce
- 2 tbsp brown sugar
- 1 tsp smoked salt
- 1 tsp black pepper

Instructions:

1. Marinate overnight.
2. Smoke or dehydrate at 160°F for 4-6 hours.

Smoked Paprika and Honey Beef Jerky

Ingredients:

- 2 lbs beef, thinly sliced
- ½ cup soy sauce
- 2 tbsp honey
- 1 tbsp smoked paprika
- 1 tsp garlic powder
- 1 tsp black pepper

Instructions:

1. Marinate overnight.
2. Smoke at 160°F for 4-6 hours.

Lemon Thyme Beef Jerky

Ingredients:

- 2 lbs beef, thinly sliced
- ½ cup fresh lemon juice
- 2 tbsp soy sauce
- 1 tbsp fresh thyme leaves
- 1 tsp garlic powder
- 1 tsp black pepper

Instructions:

1. Marinate overnight.
2. Dehydrate at 160°F for 4-6 hours.

Mediterranean Herb Beef Jerky

Ingredients:

- 2 lbs beef, thinly sliced
- ½ cup olive oil
- ¼ cup red wine vinegar
- 1 tbsp oregano
- 1 tbsp rosemary
- 1 tsp black pepper
- 1 tsp garlic powder

Instructions:

1. Marinate overnight.
2. Smoke or dehydrate at 160°F for 4-6 hours.

www.ingramcontent.com/pod-product-compliance
Lightning Source LLC
LaVergne TN
LVHW062051070526
838201LV00080B/2577